Dark Sky Question

BARNARD NEW WOMEN POETS SERIES

Edited by Claudia Rankine

LARISSA SZPORLUK

Dark Sky Question

With an Introduction by Brenda Hillman

BEACON PRESS · BOSTON

Beacon Press
25 Beacon Street
Boston, Massachusetts 02108-2892
www.beacon.org

Beacon Press books
are published under the auspices of
the Unitarian Universalist Association of Congregations.

03 02 01 00 99 98   8 7 6 5 4 3 2 1

This book is printed on recycled acid-free paper that contains at least 20 percent
postconsumer waste and meets the uncoated paper ANSI/NISO specifications for
permanence as revised in 1992.

Text design by Elizabeth Elsas
Composition by Wilsted & Taylor Publishing Services

Library of Congress Cataloging-in-Publication Data

Szporluk, Larissa.
    Dark sky question / Larissa Szporluk ; with an introduction by Brenda Hillman.
        p.   cm. — (Barnard new women poets series)
    ISBN 0-8070-6845-4
    I. Title. II. Series.
    PS3569.Z66D37   1998
    811 .54—dc21
    97-39078

FOR MY MOTHER

Contents

Introduction

MINIMALISM IN CONTEMPORARY POETRY MAKES ITS CLAIMS
on ecstatic metaphysical traditions as a single-lane dirt road makes
its way through newly barren fields on which perfect clouds have
cast perfect shadows. The enjoyment of such poetry—the type of
enjoyment that is not contingent upon happiness—helps us to en-
dure the agitation set up between the willful too-little and the help-
less too-much. Among those who bear the dream, who endure its
difficulties in the tradition of the short, mysterious lyric, is Larissa
Szporluk in her first collection.

I offer this description: Szporluk's book is composed of forty-
one mostly brief meditations. Metaphor meets metaphor in ruth-
less fashion, often with no interstitial padding, though Szporluk
frequently juxtaposes revelation achieved in quietude—as if a calm,
not very monastic yet somewhat world-renouncing saint-type were
speaking—to flinty shards of story or description. The "subject" of
the poems is mainly language, although Szporluk is not in the line
of Language poets, and her use of language is not meant to be "ex-
perimental" at the level of syntactical exploration—the sentences
are fairly straight forward, and there is no reliance on strategies like
fragmentation and pastiche. Nonetheless, she creates an animate
new universe out of cryptic original speech.

A look at how the poems are built reveals a "French braid"
effect; besides being tripartite in action—metaphysics, description,
narration or exposition—they bring in additional material from the
side, so they end up a different three than they started with. Szpor-
luk's poems are spare, withholding; they fend off the lyrical with

suspicious care. There are no continuous narratives in the poems, no "personalities" in the conventional sense, though a loose, unhinged "I" speaks many of the lines. There are also no chunks of scientific material, no rigid measures, no philosophical positioning, though their occasions are metaphysical longing for transcendent and bodily release, and the elusive search for how things work. Because the connections between observations seem tenuous, the attention to the "between"—in the form of discursiveness or subjectivity—is left out. Or, it is both left out, and is the only locus for memory and desire. She opens "Menace of the Skies" like this:

> It's a golden prison. The light on my hair
> cries for memory, for anything
> to weigh it down. All this time
> I've been hanging, the secret tides
> of my body staying high.

By making "it's" antecedent-less (or by making the antecedent both "post-cedent" and rather indefinite—tying the prison to the light and to the hair) Szporluk acknowledges the very hovering-between quality that makes existence an angel, a messenger, back and forth. Who speaks these lines? A barely human speaker, interfaced with pure tone.

I find this tone over and over again. It's a comfort, a disturbance, a voice that subverts both happening and plot: "All things which are soft become soft," she writes in "Biology of Heaven."

"The rain, who has a father, / the rain and the father are soft. / Their hour has come / to subduce the alluvial plain, / sloe eyes, black feathers and all. / They turn everything soft." Trappings of primitive mythmaking abound; here, images of the divine flirt with those of the demonic. I'm fascinated by how Szporluk achieves this slightly vatic tonality—"slightly vatic" may be an oxymoron like "somewhat unique," but Szporluk does it—without losing the sense of an ultimately intimate vision. The vision is not of an afterlife at all but of an ominous softness which opposing principles (in this case, they are called "father" and "rain") both collude with and precede. The language of the poem is not comfortable, transparent or eager to point past itself, to the "real world." "All these birds without birdness," she writes later in the poem, as if specific instances could be stripped of their essences and not be damaged, though the result might be a pure existential loneliness: "One lone voice chokes on its obstinance— / *I'm human, I'm human, I know that I know.*"

The darkness of this vision is somehow not so much frightening, portentous, or apocalyptic as purely factual. The black, the blue, disappear into the eventuality that a divine order may exist but not care, notice, or alleviate suffering. In "Holy Ghost" the speaking presence takes over the "role" of God without defining itself in the deific or the transcendent: "But where I am is so large. / You are a fly. / You are impossible." And in "Solar Wind": "I don't know what else / is on your beard. / It would be mercy, God. // I grow weird in the field."

A metaphysical poetry that shakes up the idea of the speaker as a knowable subject is bound to be a restless one. The tradition has multiple roots; Herbert comes to mind, though Szporluk inherits her "stance" less from the metaphysical poets than from a kind of force field that moves between the romantic and the early modernist traditions, arriving, after a dark fertile Coleridgean thrashing, at a muted postmodernism that allows more for disjunction as technique than for irony as point-of-view. In "Ignis Fatuus" she writes,

> I can't cope in the bog light.
> I was made big and not great.
>
> Moths swarmed in from the plains,
> wings of all sizes.
>
> And to think that I did the same,
> half-cry of a star
>
> whose boundaries were torn . . .

Finally, she both never gives in to and absolutely gives in to joy, to the ecstatic—by speeding things up and by saying as little as possible. She leaves things out in order to know more—to know more about knowing less. An epistemology is always the erotic slave to method. In these poems, when things come out of things, reversals of cause and effect occur, or the vast inwardness pushes out its shadowy flower—language foregrounded as purely as possible, however abstract and symbolic—we get simultaneously central but shifting pleasures from an unpredictable universe.

Brenda Hillman

Dark Sky Question

I

And it seemed that a lot of new worlds were forming. There was music everywhere and rhythm and beauty. But the plans were always thwarted.

ANTON BOISEN, *Out of the Depths*

Flight of the Mice

It was a small dream, like our dream,
built on the small wish to be home
once the home had been broken,
leveled by misunderstanding, by dodging,
by the loud brunt of dark, and it broke
all the plans and the ferns and soft earth
they had known, so they ran for the end
of the grasses, as you ran out of threats,
your voice a torn wire fence without land
to enclose, a disobeyed boundary,
shaking to remember where it had owned.
No one sees what they'll need to survive.
No one sees the dream thicken and rise
like the old foundation, the pieces of life
that were good, that stood the strong weather,
the one with the other, us, inside,
that intrudes on you now as you reach
what they reached, a waste as effaced as the sky,
their eyes overworked with their fabulous
loss, concrete as the race against time.

Krell

He arrives and looks around,
and doesn't know the word for wind,
and wind is the subject.

He finds a girl on a fence
hurting herself with a nail.
He pulls her away without speaking,

to her surprise, and wipes
the stuff from her hair that smells
like burning-out lights,

and suddenly it's not a burden
to be walking with her
in enemy land. When she tells him

"the best thing here is the moon,"
he feels happier than if he'd seen it
and remembers a parable

about a string that never meets
its ends, and she tells him then
about a warm place at the end

of a grove of horned trees.
If the night steadies, if it controls
their speed, they'll reach it

together, fusing in the meantime,
discarding all the nuance
that betrays them with disease.

Mauvaises Terres

The world could only be a ship,
a hunted thing to the pale light,
a swerving single body,
broken in the act and in the echo
of suggestion. With her strange fidelity
to dead and lonely sunsets, she heads
for what the dreamer in the dark
had first intended, airless chasms,
smiling depressions. If there had been
a chance, an intelligence, floating
in the wake, if only it had whispered
with the integer of a voice,
or finger, *Don't let me down*,
Earth would have heard the sound
unfinished mother, and reared her prow
in wonder that this was her son, *wait,*
that his life would urge legends,
it's my turn, of the love she had made.

Secrets of Jove

All he had to do was look down
and the river would start churning,
a little pain at first on the surface,
a little restraint. And he would swim
through the weeds and the weeds
would accommodate his motion,
bowing all over, the way a face
conforms to the sun by reddening.
And his strokes were like long knives
that left scars on the life under water,
and as everything fell into place,
it was a place exhausted by terror,
fertility barely breathing, the air
too haunted. He waded out to his
knees where her hair still fought,
and threw it as hard as he could.
There was no more moon, only space
in the waves, like a vow unmade,
or a cage whose interior flew.

Libido

A hand has her hair.
Don't move, don't cry out—
The odd foliage is shining in the light.

With the stealth of a wheel,
he rams against her knees
from behind. She falls

back into his purpose,
which is hers: to be provided for,
to find her insides altered

and grow huge.
But he runs off, done with her mouth,
leaving her dazed by the waste

of that kind of love.
She asks around, asks how,
where do we feel to find who we are,

watches some poppies freeze
in an orgy of plants,
their cold red gaze grown sideways.

She listens to parrots,
true inner birds, never at rest,
into whose breasts the world

blows pleasure,
shaking like nests full of Indian bees—
To scream is to sing.

Allegro of the Earth

It takes many doves to make a woman.
I've been chasing them forever
as they drift through summer unexplained.
Like the need in certain sounds
to be fulfilling, they repeat each year
blue fields, blue frost, far north,
ferried across gulfs,
in search of the torturer's house;
miles away, he unlocks his clear interior door.
I lose them to him every time.
Don't cry. Be warm. Watch how.
And as he changes them completely,
peeling them down
to the hollow that resides at the center
of all of them, a piccolo hole,
the sole shape of his desire,
a hollow that listens,
shivers, ringing the dim light,
arrested by their separated feathers,
I'm aware of one thing.

Prowler's Universe

i

Everything is mine for a while.
Her chest gives pause to what her life is.
I could use a stick to make it louder.

I could be her family, lift her by the hips
from this roof and watch her fly,
borne by the lie of trust

between us—there is no pond,
no wreck, no bottom. . . .
The smear that is her cheek,

sidelong, sedate,
rides the surface near the shore now.
I feel her with my knees:

She grows big like glass and I
am spring and the mind
is just the woman we're all after.

ii

In the beginning, she is afraid
of the cattle.
They are not from the heart.
They shake a little rain or something on her face.

She twitches from sounds that pass
through her blood
of a faraway, then close, then far, entourage.
Not a colorful xylophone sound

but hard, like a game
under stadium lights. When the land jerks,
she jerks, moist and reddish,
with the land . . .

gets used to the licking,
throws her pants up like a kite—
her smile survives.
No era is spared the site of her lips

as she gives, smiling,
her body's tiny organisms
to occidental winds
to be ruptured. *Do good. Serve. Give.*

iii
For five minutes,
there was dust—of voices,
structures within structures,
cosmos, whatever it was,
the face it cost.

When will I give up
my love of pain?
When I am equal to the whole world.
When I roll over,
and the empty sky is perfect.

II

Was long in holy shudders; yet at the same time in a deep sleep.
Thought whether anything holy was about to appear. Seemed
to me as if I was cast upon my face; but cannot certify this.

Swedenborg's Journal of Dreams

.

Holy Ghost

All my thoughts of you are good ones.
The horse whose neck is clothed with thunder—
they are good ones.
*The voice that shakes the wilderness—*good ones.
I think about how, if I could wake up,
I could go to your life,
how that would be good, if I could wake up.

But where I am is so large.
You are a fly.
You are impossible.

Where I am is so large, like a dark saying,
repeating. Where I am
is repeating. I don't know where it begins.

Where I am is the same,
but the light just takes you away, and I
am the only one here.
It's mine, like a dark saying—
Hide them in the dust together.

Bind their faces in secret.
You see how it's mine? You see how I try
to wake up?
The horse whose neck is clothed with thunder—
they were good ones.

I am the only one here, a giant,
asleep on the damp floor.
I am on the floor
of my invention, my forest
of dark sayings—
the Lord shall hiss.

My forest is always the same.
I am asleep on the damp floor.
My lids are down. Your face is a secret.
Hiss, hiss.

Age of Piracy

They reach through her brow
to tear out the trees
they think she dreams about,
the balanced land she left behind,
and throw her boat back,
empty, to him she left behind,
and laugh at her mistake,
that she could fly on and on,
out of their sight and knowledge.
And they laugh into life
beyond themselves, as she, obsessed,
stares up at the dipping sky,
past the spreading pitch, telling herself,
I am that high, and they laugh
as they open what they stole,
seeing nothing was in her but sea
and the long tedium of falling,
lost in her green and winding galleries,
tucks and turns, and they laugh,
wings in their teeth beating backwards.

Ghost Continent

It's a lot like emptiness, the season
of dying fish, black drink,
the person you loved best, and left,
giving off light in the recession.
It would have startled the fire user,
who towered over nature,
this material you're passing through
to save a little of, like a radio.
Paddle faster. Skim across the giant
things in hiding, blow on the sick.
The deep returns a makeshift
surface, wake, blue-tarred road.
Miles from here (but you're gone)
the wrong land will be discovered.

A Cappella

They were lying in the shoreline
foam, navels
trapping sand, eyes open
on the pebbles and the tiny spiral
shells, and he turned to him and said,
Did you love much?

He squeezed a slippy sea grub.
Not much.

And it was quiet. Undivided
quiet. Even the great
claws of tide
tore into them in silence.

This is how it is, they guessed,
to run out of fresh
ideas . . .

Heed the jellyfish, the first man mouthed,
Float more still-ly.
But his words weren't loud,

and the other man grabbed it,
a fat one, lilac,
and everything formerly dumb
broke—like divas
into octaves as he underwent alone.

Vapor

Sometimes the monks perspire
inside those woolen cloaks.
When you see them hold pigeons,
their hands glisten. This means
acceptance of death, dew
on their throats in the morning,
snow that can rain or simply
make love with itself. And they
will go there. And the things
around them will be crying.

Ignis Fatuus

I can't cope in the bog light.
I was made big and not great.

Moths swarmed in from the plains,
wings of all sizes.

And to think that I did the same,
half-cry of a star

whose boundaries were torn,
then your special way of walking

on the peels. Beautiful voiceless things
were boiled alive.

For three thousand days, I asked you
to stop it.

Little girls are scarcer now.
There won't be a second bride.

Who could go on trying?
Victims form a line even God doesn't know,

their desire for home
snuffed out like a phantom.

I'll catch silk in the night wind instead,
narrations of our baby.

Part of the sky is all of the sky.
The rest is wasted.

Menace of the Skies

It's a golden prison. The light on my hair
cries for memory, for anything
to weigh it down. All this time
I've been hanging, the secret tides
of my body staying high. I remember
I am childless. I would have given it
a hunter's name, Orion, because that's where
we end, up here, in these wisps.
We didn't do right by the Earth.
It kept giving us pictures, big frantic snow,
midnight fires in the willows.
We should have walked somewhere like Jesus,
sowing equilibrium, slow to consume.
We should have fought to know him,
to trap and spawn his grace.
But maybe we'd already met, and he *saw*,
and this is the scar of that encounter.

Radiolaria

Maybe the earth where her house is
is dangerous,
the foundation easing away.

She's out of the man.
Bereavement means travel, nearly,
a plane with no wings,

her face on the rug,
moment of confusion:
But I asked him to leave,

he was stretching. . . .
Slush in the lowlands.
It must have been an old

attachment. Something
outside of her is thinking,
I didn't even feel him;

she was drawn down.
Her vowels went dark.
Her body rowed back

to a time when loss
was not yet architecture,
but still on the eyes

as the weight that would make
her want to build,
when rocks opened up,

and small lives within,
and within, opened up,
until their skins filled the water,

and rose to the sun realm.
Maybe she rose with them,
and landed here, as they flew on,

and like their broken skeletons,
she's staying flat
to grow elaborate again.

Slander from the Inner Nests

Leaps between trees in the dark
are felt far away by those
not connected to the forest, the springing
of curved feet, trembling reactions of plant life.
People pounce in their sleep
when the thing lets go of the old one,
grips the skin of the next,
its body riding the trunk, clenched inside,
the joint contortion of a couple.
The forests are tilting, forests of riders, forests
maimed at the waist from the strain
of centuries of monkeys, forests swished,
forests thrashed, forests stripped in the rush—
our canopies, God, the dome above
glowering with water.

III

The greatest defeat, in anything, is to forget, and above all to forget what it is that smashed you, and to let yourself be smashed . . .

LOUIS-FERDINAND CÉLINE, *Journey to the End of the Night*

Io Remembers

There is no sound at all on this wild upland.
The horses have stopped falling
in their great arc through the air.
The panic that carried their necks over the crag
became, early on, in their legs, regret.
The dark knowing that spoils the morning
enters them now, showing them how,
like a difference in contour, they weren't the real
power of the field. How their bearing was minor,
their bones meaning more to the earth
than what each aloof mane in the wind had been.
Their eyes, which before were clear, crowd
with the fleas madness brings, as she notes
in the noonday heat how each part lies,
spread across rock, like her own in that scene,
half-girl, half-cow, the cloud half off.

Crocodilia

The air yellows
with the energy of grief.
He touches her eyes, almost humming.
What are those depths
to which we all disappear?
Seas advance and recede.
Ebb and flow. Mountains are lifted
and leveled. *Ebb and flow.*
A mosaic of tiny bones
shifts a bit in the heat.
There are two kinds of time, side by side;
tears bind them.
His finger rests on her lips, then goes in.
Extinction sucks the tip,
softly biting.

Solar Wind

I don't pray.
I just walk out there
where it's thin
with my bow and aim.

But I should have yelled.
I should have changed the world.

A person can die of balance,
just gleam like squid
and disappear.

The fence around our house
is soft with rain.
It can't stop my arrows.
It can't stop

what wants to happen,
the meteors I hear, power lines
blowing from the mountain,

or the girl somewhere
who reads you,
whose skin has memorized your life.
Nothing stops her fingers;
they swim with you at night.

Leave if you're leaving.
Leave plain mud.

I don't know what else
is on your beard.
It would be mercy, God.

I grow weird in the field.

Occupant of the House

Someday the phoebe bird will sing.
The sword grass will rise like corn.
I will be free and not know from what.
Like a pure wild race
captured for science, too wronged
to go back, too strange to be damaged,
my fierceness has disappeared.
If it doesn't end soon, the pain will dilute,
the sin turn to sheen in the garden,
your routine a genial rain.
And I would get up from my special chair
and swim through the soundproof ceiling,
its material soft and blue,
a threshold to mobile worlds.
I wouldn't know about my body.
If it were winter, winter would tingle,
summer would burn,
like the lamp in my ear that bristles like fire
when you examine the drum—
is it hot? *I don't know.*
A shell malnourished by darkness,
a great fish charmed into injury, I swallow
the wires, the hours, the shock.
You knew what the sky would mean to me.

Under the Bridge

You never know when somebody will
stick a little knife
in your heart and walk away—

and the handle that smells of his hand
vibrates by your breast
as he ducks through the trees

and minutes later blows like a shirt pin
across the frozen lake.
And you're all wet, and he's in love

with what he's done.
And because of the cut,
the distance of your life pours out,

and because of the clouds
like fat that surround you,
you don't hear

for a long time
the tom-tom beating
in the sky, letting shadows

too heavy to be birds,
and yelling with a message
to forgive him

like the others did their father
under that bridge there
where ropes still linger

in remembrance of their necks,
where a flute in its case lies cold—
forgive him. Say

his name. It was only
power that he had to have,
and look what the one thrust gave him.

Benefits of Drowning

The light has been so awful.
Not whipped as a child,
I'm scared of human power.
They say there is an end
but I go round and round
with unscrupulous desires
in regions of my throat.
Nests smell from neglect.
Autumn will smell too
if the summer wasn't good.
Hard rain brings exaltation.
All the little mouths come out,
blowing rings of brightness.
I can enter them, not stagger,
not a skeleton, not plagued,
not by ghosts.

Envoy of the Boat

He loves what he cannot love,
lapping toward it, with the love
that exists between lakes, wanting each other
so much, wanting just to meet
inside themselves, taste the fish,
how deep is your gulch,
how vocal the fowl that visit you?
With unexpected tenderness,
that's how he lives, watching,
dreaming at night they grow close,
the forlorn part of their bodies
upswelling with swell, each pore frothed too,
morning forgotten, the message, war,
more sky in his mouth than water.

Small Lions

The crux of love, any love,
is what will hold. Within
the mold of water, emotionally
quiet, nibbled brow,

he slides out, part creek
and things that drink, part
ghost, part holster.
He can't remember how

she crossed the floor,
what filled her thighs. *Is it
really October?* She looks up,
about to be touched,

in wonder, like the round
belly of a jar. October.
He wants to turn the trees down,
restore year zero,

spare her knees the separation,
lack of sleep, keep
the language in her heart
from coming out

somewhere along a road;
if he could float, he might find
members of the next world,
with their eyes.

IV

The inward skies of man will accompany him across any void
upon which he ventures and will be with him to the end of time.
There is just one way in which that inward world differs from
outer space. It can be more volatile and mobile, more terrible and
impoverished, yet withal more ennobling in its self-consciousness,
than the universe that gave it birth.

LOREN EISELEY, *The Unexpected Universe*

Biology of Heaven

All things which are soft become soft.
The rain, who has a father,
the rain and the father are soft.
Their hour has come
to subduce the alluvial plain,
sloe eyes, black feathers and all.
They turn everything soft.

Up here, without support, the totality
of light is frightening.
Its lunge exceeds the enemy's,
its appetite the cannibal's.
Why can't eternity
be where they were, back in the chain,
the pull for the worm,
scrape with the carnivore,
the feeling of constant attraction forever?
Not this airy regularity.
Not this luminous branchlessness.
There is nothing to study.
The anxiety reaches a pitch.
All these birds without birdness,
way too free to sing, give in.
One lone voice chokes on its obstinance—
I'm human, I'm human, I know that I know.

Agnosia

A far star is making leaves.
Someday they might brush this place,
their ordinary fire

tittering around us.
The porches are locked at dusk.
A piece could be out there.

But you should think less,
how you threw yourself on her back,
and the voice of the wharf's

weak-looking birds cried
more than it had to, her dark red dress
falling ill. You blew

all the animals away,
and never stopped feeling their dirt.
You ran after her too,

for a year, on your skeleton foot
over the hollow ice,
to prove to yourself

what was left
the cannibal wind would be finishing
up, the tail end

of her solved in the sky,
how an enemy bends,
a girl, waterjug, edges adjusting in time.

Mother of Days

The rock is the agony
it can't cry out
when that great warm thing sun
goes down, the grass all gone
into black oceanology.
Nothing beautiful about its leaving.
Nothing true about the wife
who's falling in the crater
that formed outside her house;
but she feels that there is one,
that it is her own sore
that has swallowed her up,
and like the rock, that she is stung
by the riddle of such brief light.

The sky is just a phantom now
brushing through the trees
that crackle in the sour heat.
The branches sway with ants
that nest in the outer bark
behind dark round holes, and they sway
with the old forest's sorrow,
old noise of the beginning
that had draped them once
with density, hanging animals and steam;
swaying, they keep begging

every bygone second for release—
But who would you be? asks the universe.
Not this. Not this body.

Koan

You cross a broken field.
Mirror, mirror.
There's a scarecrow in a dress.

Sometimes I know
I won't see you again.
It's a bad place

to get emotional, alone
in the car, haze pouring
through the valley.

But I see you on your knees,
I see everything,
her stick arms pull you

to her skirt, hens
seeking shelter, I hear
crying. I hear crying

as the only true noise,
a chorus of tearing ice,
the dead straw

she is made of
crying, crows caught
in the sky, a duct

of her odd world;
in your rush to get in,
you bruise the shape

of your being.
This window I look out of
traps my breath

until nothing I pound
isn't part mine,
and black-and-blue inside.

Orchard of Far Worlds

This is the land of small rain.
Because it is round, I still need you.
The men move amongst their stones.
Because it is holy, the air is uneasy
with memories of things that are gone,
bats whirling out of the trees,
a cobra's slow-rising hood,
mangoes that ambered the blood.
You should have gone further.
There are pockets given to frost
where portions of birds lie frozen.
Where the outside extends to within
on a vein that cuts itself open.
Where minerals fail in the quiet
to live otherwise than rich,
and jade keeps revealing its strings,
mica, more fragile planes,
to no one, to nothing.
Where breath will suffer to be music,
where skin turns infrared—
they say you hurried for the end.
A sudden recollection lights the wind.

Axiom of Maria

Clover fills the darkness quickly,
splitting open, spreading.

It's a slightly different planet
that surrounds the same night,

an unction in the sun
that spins the Earth faster—

the couple pulls apart, turning hostile,
her body taking off into the wild,

his influence inside her,
showing, like a stripe, the same question,

Where is my palace?, asked of the mountains
beyond her dream, as if time

were on fire, peregrines, herons,
burning in everything, singed by need,

as if all the metals in the world
surfaced, blowing out of people,

carbon, sulphur, gold—
the feeling she had had while climbing

like a child suddenly old, a feeling of being
the greatest voice as it ceased,

rain hissing through her, a blue comet,
coming and going in streaks.

Eel

Then I will rest,
long, in a freeze, falling
through the life of the lake, long,
like heartbreak, long
through the element of coma,
a world of no enemies, no friends,
like an eye that won't open,
that grows long out of nowhere to look
and becomes its own place,
falling through blindness,
like a beam from the time of stars
whose death meant arrival,
and then I don't know
if I'm all that the water knew
or water is all I was,
if falling is falling backwards,
falling out of love,
like sound falling back into silence
as if swallowed by bog,
a bog that hangs in the balance
before swallowing God.

V

We know this to be true; we should moderate ourselves, but we are furiously carried . . .

ROBERT BURTON, *The Anatomy of Melancholy*

A Line to Mars

It begins with a line to Mars,
to its far red innocence,
to the eyes on it, theirs and ours, far dream
of far life, better than us,
she will go far. And the dust tells
of her arrival, the day her foot touched,
the race that rushed to her side,
hands that couldn't wait to feel this far thing
from that star. And the dust tells
of the rumble that followed all afternoon
in the far red air, the bodies that loved her,
spreading her senseless, begging thinly out loud.
How it wasn't love in our book,
but love on Mars, how she died all wet
in their shadows, died far, died far,
her voice in the sizzling dust, whispering
conscience—something she'd thought on Earth,
but couldn't cross the barrier,
something that burst into flame,
desire, a crowd, surrounding her without one.

Harness

What if the sun sent wind to kill things
it couldn't kill itself,

and the wind struck hard,
smelling of grass on fire,

and stirred your ears before doing you in,
so the last thing you heard

was deceit, *what things, what things,*
the breath of unraveling love,

the word *half*, half-grass, half-fire.
Half-torn in the clouds,

half-sated, you were lulled by the sound
of carriage, pulled by the waist,

then raised, a gift, to the hottest place,
life's dark weight

sublimed into violet.
Call it dying well, the spell of family

broken. Call it facile,
missing no one, no devotion,

tossing all your bindings, all your shackles,
bareback on your loose assassin.

Death by a Thousand Cuts

The human body is transparent,
the heart an underwater flower
that can't be reached through the waves.
You can look through your fingers at the sun.
Like the little fish Echeneis who curbs the violence of the wind,
your hand can turn your hatred
into smoke. Keep waving
at your husband. Feel the sizzling.
The smoke becomes radiant, not a trick.
You can feel yourself dispelled in it, easily,
invisibly, the way God pierces nature to make things grow.
Compare the sulphur rivers underground,
hurling themselves in the stony dark,
with the paradise of outer space,
a flow without a vein.

The Grass and the Sin

They are waiting for it, waiting all their lives.
They are question marks, changing into feathers.
They are lost between their legs. *Desire hath no rest.*
When grass is blowing, it lives twice, as grass and waves.
When they're in love, they give themselves to prophecies
and tongues, clouds that come with clear instructions.
Forty days and forty nights. . . . There is soundness in it,
soundness in her thighs, scrape, grind. They are waiting
to run down. They are hot. There are brilliant colors
in the sea, so deep no one sees them; air hides even more.
Two of every sort. . . . If he is not her husband, but divine,
if they are found, will they be punished? With no aroma,
who will know, if he's divine. . . . If Noah's water never
came, who would know how bad the land had been . . .

Halo Formation

Wind is omen;
omen does things to the trees,

their dream of rescue fading.
Omen loves that moment, that *No*,

when the whole life leans
and the cruelty turns definite:

her arms fall away,
saying simply, *Get me*.

And omen, unknown attractor,
keeps pulling all the strings,

finding the scene exotic,
finding Diana, the injured part,

finding in the shape and feel
of so much hope, in the rubbing

and pulling, genesis, finding
in the lurid, alien hue, somebody good,

who must have been good—
what happened here was deafening,

the dangling of the changeling,
her brow in a bleed of light.

Duressor

In darkness, crabs are believed to rest.
It is nobody's world. It is even less
theirs when they touch that first
inch of beach and the stunning blow
of elastic fire that is nobody's star
knocks them out of existence,
knocking them out like knees
in a murderous arena of tungsten lamps
and questioners. Of tables and pounding
fists. Of the decision of tide
to rebel against attraction, flattening out,
the moon looking up in surprise
from the underside of the stagnant water,
twisted and sad, like a coroner's eye
scrambled in a dearth of time,
the faraway body's insomnia, the crabs
combing the sand without minds.

Euphoria of Rope

When all voices cease
and the waters are still,
what is left to be afraid of?

That the stasis of the head
is not alone—an invisible companion
has been waltzing all along

around it like a halo,
the secret fire of an angel,
a secondary blood with primal

circulation, and how it moves
and changes shape,
engulfing food, *to swallow*,

to renew, is how the executioner
can fly, borne across the bounds
of documented time,

horizon of the scaffold
beyond which details fade,
seeing nothing of the hood, or tools

he puts away, nothing of the cord,
which is external, his energy
diffused, cord that is immortalized

from youth to youth, and how it moves
and changes shape, engulfing food,
to swallow, to renew,

is how the sky persuades the Earth
to keep her burning center
undisclosed, microscopic vapors

moistening her face,
like snakebreath on the egg—
we would die again to know.

Deliverer

No one can spin forever.
It will all slow down.
The poles will grow sore on the world,
the valve in the heart
will retard, *slow down, slow down,*
to a speed we can't see,
can't feel, slow as a cloud
carting snow through atomic darkness,
slow as the milk she can't send
to her son, when the magnet
is low, when the blood,
can't see, can't feel, how slow . . .
as the whale pulling out of the sea
can't see the no-sea,
can't feel the tide bring it back,
breaking her agony over the beach,
who she was, who she loved,
who God opened up, *how still and how slow,*
belly no longer with Jonah.

The Corals

Below man, below hearing,
below the ghostly movement,
they are growing.

Below the splendor
and tether of a spawning domain,
they grow.

Without sky, without goal,
without children to feel
of their own, they grow rosy

and odd, like a cloud in the head,
drawing the water's spectra,
turning everything dead

into edifice, the plain floor
mountainous, founding a home
for the end of the animal form,

a skeletal welcome,
shrine to the endocrine:
these are the tombs of the sea,

growing huge in the prodigal
deep, where a life comes around
to empty its backbone.

Sanctuary

Who loves the world? The sleeper does.
Where he is, the jungle is still large.
The things that sing, sing flight into his heart,
and sky, and sun, and sounds so glad
he thinks his mother was a bird,
but singing, warn him, as she didn't,
of the scourge to come, and feed him,
not as she did, warm against her plumes,
thistles, moths and worms,
but a hundred false beginnings
so the true one will be watered down,
will barely hurt him, scourge,
the true one, whose coming will ignite
like Babylon the great, in whose hold
he'll perish like a river in a cherished bed,
slowly turning pebbles, tossing mud
and weed, and fling himself
at last, like parrots leaving trees
for cages made of brass, too fresh and green,
too real once, to dream of real things.

Acknowledgments

GRATEFUL ACKNOWLEDGMENT IS MADE TO THE EDITORS OF the following journals, in which these poems first appeared: *AGNI*: "Ghost Continent," "Harness"; *Boston Book Review*: "Slander from the Inner Nests," "Crocodilia"; *Cokefish*: "Vapor"; *Englynion*: "Benefits of Drowning"; *Grand Street*: "Holy Ghost," "Flight of the Mice," "Occupant of the House," "Eel"; *Harvard Review*: "Envoy of the Boat," "Allegro of the Earth"; *Hayden's Ferry Review*: "Mauvaises Terres"; *Indiana Review*: "Ignis Fatuus," "Koan," "Radiolaria," "Krell"; *Jeopardy*: "Small Lions"; *Lullwater Review*: "Libido," "Age of Piracy"; *Mid-American Review*: "Death by a Thousand Cuts," "Menace of the Skies," "Duressor"; *Northwest Review*: "Prowler's Universe"; *Poem*: "A Cappella"; *Poet Lore*: "Agnosia"; *Santa Monica Review*: "Under the Bridge"; *Virginia Quarterly Review*: "Io Remembers," "Axiom of Maria," "Halo Formation."

Special thanks to Askold Melnyczuk and Fiona McCrae for featuring many of these poems in *Take Three 1: AGNI New Poets Series*, Graywolf Press, 1996, and to the Millay Colony for the Arts for their flawless accommodation.

I am indebted to my teachers and friends, without whom these poems would have neither evolved nor mattered, to Brenda Hillman for selecting them, to Don Foster for his humor and support, and, finally, to my husband and my son for their unwavering love.